Richard Burton

Lyrics of Brotherhood

Richard Burton

Lyrics of Brotherhood

ISBN/EAN: 9783743351219

Manufactured in Europe, USA, Canada, Australia, Japa

Cover: Foto ©Thomas Meinert / pixelio.de

Manufactured and distributed by brebook publishing software (www.brebook.com)

Richard Burton

Lyrics of Brotherhood

LYRICS
OF BROTHERHOOD

RICHARD BURTON

BOSTON
SMALL, MAYNARD & COMPANY
M DCCC XCIX

Copyright, 1899, by
Small, Maynard & Company.
(Incorporated.)

Entered at Stationers' Hall.

Rockwell and Churchill Press
Boston, U.S.A.

Due acknowledgments are made to the editors of the Atlantic, *the* Century, Harper's Magazine, *the* Cosmopolitan, *the* Bookman, *the* Critic, *the* Independent, *and the* Outlook *for permission to reprint poems originally appearing in those publications.*

Contents

	Page
BLACK SHEEP	3
"THE MORN IS FINE"	4
THE WORLD PLAY	5
THE HUMAN TOUCH	7
NOSTALGIA	8
OLD SONGS	9
THE FOREFATHER	10
TO—MORROW AND TO—DAY	12
THE POLAR QUEST	13
WAR NOTES:	
I FALSE PEACE AND TRUE	14
II EXTRAS	14
III PRO PATRIA MORI	15
IV PARADES	16
V DECORATION DAY	17
THE SPHINX	18
CITIES OF ELD	20
A CHOPIN PRELUDE	23
THE WAYS RETURN	24
THE ELEMENTAL JOYS	25
THE NORTH LIGHT	26
LIGHT AND SHADE	28
CHILD—PLAY	29
LIFE	30
THE ETERNAL FEMININE	31
A WESTERN SCENE	32
THE MODERN SAINT	33
SEALED ORDERS	34
BLACK OAKS	35
HAYING TIME	36

CHANGELESS	*Page* 37
" IN SPEAKING OF THE LITTLE ONES WE LOVE "	38
GOSPELS	39
TRAVEL	40
THE QUEST OF SUMMER	41
ON THE LINE	48
CLEAR HEAVENS	50
TWO BARDS	51
PLAINT OF THE PINE	52
TRAGEDIES	53
FLASHES	54
LAUREL	55
MARY MAGDALEN	56
PICTURES	57
THE DREAM AND THE WAKING	58
LIFE AND SONG	59
INTERPRETATION	60
THE NATIONAL AIR	61
A PRELUDE	62
IN THE GRASS	63
THE POET TO THE CLOUD	64
A STORM	65
THE LILY	66
THE MUSIC STRAIN	67
A MADRIGAL	68
GYPSIES	69
A LEGEND OF THE MOON	70

Lyrics of Brotherhood

BLACK SHEEP

FROM their folded mates they wander far,
  Their ways seem harsh and wild;
They follow the beck of a baleful star,
  Their paths are dream-beguiled.

Yet haply they sought but a wider range,
  Some loftier mountain-slope,
And little recked of the country strange
  Beyond the gates of hope.

And haply a bell with a luring call
  Summoned their feet to tread
Midst the cruel rocks, where the deep pitfall
  And the lurking snare are spread.

Maybe, in spite of their tameless days
  Of outcast liberty,
They're sick at heart for the homely ways
  Where their gathered brothers be.

And oft at night, when the plains fall dark
  And the hills loom large and dim,
For the Shepherd's voice they mutely hark,
  And their souls go out to him.

Meanwhile, "Black sheep! Black sheep!" we cry,
  Safe in the inner fold;
And maybe they hear, and wonder why,
  And marvel, out in the cold.

"THE MORN IS FINE"

THE morn is fine, the wind smells sweet;
   The nomad man that lurks in me
Arouses, and I fain would meet
   The fellowship of vagrancy

Along the mountain roads of day.
   Hail, foot-farers from near and far;
Ye who do love the wandering way
   Of Beauty, show what stuff ye are,

And face the westward-luring path:
   The hours are yours 'twixt dawn and night;
And since that Youth's sure aftermath
   Is Memory — use the day aright,

That by the fire, when evening's here,
   Your cronies gathered close around,
The old-time deeds may twinkle clear,
   And peace be in the back-log's sound.

THE WORLD PLAY
("AND ALL THE MEN AND WOMEN MERELY PLAYERS")

THE entrance-price you willy-nilly pay,
   Sit with your kind, take pleasure, if you may,
Or puzzle at the meaning of the play.

Comedy

The humors of the time, the painted show
Of character, the Attic salt of wit;
Now, laughter lifts it high, now, tender woe
For a pale moment o'er the stage must flit,
To make the main plot merrier; maids and men
Teach life is sweet and love may come again.

Melodrama

See how the swashbucklers swagger!
   Hark to the villain's dark cry!
Much is a-doing and many are ruing.
   Innocents, destined to die,
Haply, with thrust of a dagger.
Evil frustrate and virtue tried and true,
Romance, adventure, sleight, and derring-do,
The earth's wide passions served up hot for you!

Farce

See the buffoon's fat cheeks ballooning out!
Thwack! the lath sword descends, guffaws are
   rife
'Midst gallery gods, with many a boorish shout
Of approbation. Yet, 'tis part of life,

And honest too, — the grammarless, crude heart
Of one's own kinsmen, and this stir-about
Is wholesome, though it lack the soul of art.

Tragedy

Slow evolution to a fateful close ;
Deepest of dramas knocking at our soul ;
Glints of the gay, but gloom that spreads and
   grows
Towards some sardonic end, the gruesome goal
Of all the light, the motion, and the glee
      Pranked out high-heartedly.
Behind man's quest and woman's sacrifice,
Bravery and risk and lure of ardent eyes,
      Quieting the stir,
Mingling mould-odors with love's sweetest myrrh,
Forever looms and glooms the sepulchre !

Epilogue

Great Watcher of the whole, the motley shift
Of play and counterplay, sole Critic, who
Must understand, because Creator too ;
Prompter and playwright both : the curtains lift
And fall, while joy and sorrow interweave ;
We know full well what time to smile or grieve,
No more ; the ultimate meaning's shut from view.
The world-play act by act moves on, and we
Are shaken by its moods, — mirth, anguish,
   mystery.

THE HUMAN TOUCH

HIGH thoughts and noble in all lands
    Help me; my soul is fed by such.
But ah, the touch of lips and hands, —
        The human touch!
Warm, vital, close, life's symbols dear, —
These need I most, and now, and here.

NOSTALGIA

ALL through their lives men build or dream them homes,
   Longing for peace and quiet and household love ;
All through their lives — though offering hecatombs
   To worldly pleasures and the shows thereof.

And at the last, life-sick, with still the same
   Unconquerable desire within their breast,
They yearn for heaven and murmur its dear name,
   Deeming it, more than mortal homes are, blest.

OLD SONGS

THERE is many a simple song one hears,
To an outworn tune, that starts the tears ;
Not for itself — for the buried years.

Perchance 'twas heard in the days of youth,
When breath was buoyant and words were truth ;
When joys were peddled at Life's gay booth.

Or maybe it sounded along a lane
Where She walked with you — and now again
You catch Love's cadence, Love's old sweet pain.

Or else it stole through a room where lay
A dear one dying, and seemed to say :
" Love and death, they shall pass away."

It rises out of the Long Ago,
And that is the reason it shakes you so
With pain and passion and buried woe.

There is many a simple song that brings
From deeps of living, on viewless wings,
The tender magic of bygone things.

THE FOREFATHER

HERE at the country inn,
   I lie in my quiet bed,
And the ardent onrush of armies
   Throbs and throbs in my head.

Why, in this calm, sweet place,
   Where only silence is heard,
Am I 'ware of the crash of conflict —
   Is my blood to battle stirred?

Without, the night is blessed
   With the smell of pines, with stars;
Within, is the mood of slumber,
   The healing of daytime scars.

'Tis strange — yet I am thrall
   To epic agonies:
The tumult of myriads dying
   Is borne to me on the breeze.

Mayhap in the long ago
   My forefather grim and stark
Stood in some hell of carnage,
   Faced forward, fell in the dark;

And I, who have always known
   Peace, with her dove-like ways,
Am gripped by his martial spirit
   Here in the after days.

I cannot rightly tell:
  I lie, from all stress apart,
And the ardent onrush of armies
  Surges hot through my heart.

The Forefather

TO-MORROW AND TO-DAY

TO-MORROW hath a rare, alluring sound;
To-day is very prose; and yet the twain
Are but one vision seen through altered eyes.
Our dreams inhabit one; our stress and pain
Surge through the other.   Heaven is but to-day
Made lovely with to-morrow's face, for aye.

THE POLAR QUEST

UNCONQUERABLY, men venture on the quest
   And seek an ocean amplitude unsailed,
Cold, virgin, awful. Scorning ease and rest,
   And heedless of the heroes who have failed,
They face the ice floes with a dauntless zest.

The polar quest ! Life's offer to the strong !
   To pass beyond the pale, to do and dare,
Leaving a name that stirs us like a song,
   And making captive some strange Otherwhere,
Though grim the conquest, and the labor long.

Forever courage kindles, faith moves forth
To find the mystic floodway of the North.

WAR NOTES
I False Peace and True

THERE is a peace wherein man's mood is
    tame —
Like clouds upon a windless summer day
The hours float by; the people take no shame
  In alien mocks; like children are they gay.
Such peace is craven-bought, the cost is great;
Not so is nourished a puissant state.

There is a peace amidst the shock of arms
  That satisfies the soul, though all the air
Hurtles with horror and is rude with harms;
  Life's gray gleams into golden deeds, and where,
The while swords slept, unrighteousness was done,
Wrong takes her death-blow, and from sun to sun
That clarion cry *My Country!* makes men one.

II "Extras"

THE crocuses in the Square
  Lend a winsome touch to the May;
  The clouds are vanished away,
The weather is bland and fair;
Now peace seems everywhere.
  Hark to the raucous, sullen cries:
  "Extra! Extra!" — tersely flies
  The news, and a great hope mounts, or dies.

About the bulletin-boards
   Dark knots of people surge ;
   Strained faces show, then merge
In the inconspicuous hordes
That yet are the Nation's lords.
   "Extra ! Extra ! Big fight at sea ! "
   Was the luck with us ? Is it victory ?
   Dear God, they died for you and me !

Meanwhile the crocuses down the street
With heaven's own patience are calm and sweet.

III Pro Patria Mori

AS a gold and scarlet sunset
   Glories a sombre day,
That else were all unmemoried,
   Dying in dusk away :

Great acts man's day emblazon,
   God's lilies out of life's mud ;
The splendid flower of heroes
   Out of a soil of blood.

The date of the deed ? Who recks it ?
   Such moments are timeless things.
Of old, Leonidas thrills us,
   He travels on Fame's wide wings ;

Or, blithe through the Russian bullets,
   Rushes the Light Brigade
To death — and the whole world echoes
   The sound of the charge they made.

War Notes

And now, — with the ancient valor, —
   In the clutch of a tropic sun,
Our own Rough Riders conquer,
   Though the foe be four to one.

The date of the deed? 'Tis nothing!
   Count it by tears or cheers.
For the men who die for Country
   Have naught to do with the years!

IV   PARADES

Civic Display

THE uniforms gleam bright, and bands galore
   Play up the feet that step in time full gay;
This soldiering looks handsome; hark, the roar
   That rends the very skies of Spring to-day
From mobile multitudes who line the way.
Behold the grace and gallantry of war!

The Return of the Veterans

Beneath grey gloom they tramp along: their tread
   Lacks rhythm; faded, soiled, and torn their
     dress;
They wot of storm and peril, wounds that bled,
   And pains beyond imagination's guess.
   The lookers-on, struck mute by tenderness,
Hardly huzza: it is as if the dead
   Walked with the quick. Beneath a brooding
     sky
   The bronzed and battered veterans limp by.

V Decoration Day

THE uses of adversity are sweet :
   Red war, the lust of conquest is forgot ;
Beneath bland skies a nation stays her feet,
   To laud the hero, grace his sleeping-spot ;
For every drop of blood old swords have let,
The rose, the lily, and the violet.

THE SPHINX

WHAT is her silence saying,
    As she peers from her stony eyes,
Creature of massive sternness,
    Woman of monstrous size?

Ever the ages ask it
    Of the Deity of the Sands,
And the Spirit of Egypt answers,
    The ancient one of the lands:

" Drought is my old-time menace,
    Rain brings my happy while,
I blossom forth like a garden
    With the flooding of the Nile.

" It means good grain for my people,
    Yea, life for my maids and men;
My kings in their great hewn sepulchres,
    E'en they grow joyful then.

" In the Sign of the Lion stately,
    In the Sign of the Virgin too,
Do the waters come upwelling,
    And the fields turn fair to view.

" So of old my servants builded
    The Sphinx; she rose amain,
A shape half beast, half human,
    Above the burning plain;

The Sphinx

"For a sure, eternal token
  Of reverence and praise,
A sacrifice to Father Nile
  Done in the elder days.

"And if, in Time's later lapses,
  Innumerous aliens come
To guess at her mystic semblance,
  And her front seems riddlesome,

"My race will comprehend her,
  Their goddess, and laud her high
In her worship of the waters
  Beneath a rainless sky."

CITIES OF ELD

IN the Orient uplands afar,
   Beyond the roof of the world,
Strange buried cities are,
   Where over the winds have whirled
And the Sky's bleak stormings swirled
   For century-sweeps of time.
They lie deep hid in the slime,
   Or frore in their ancient shroud,
Careless of clear or cloud, —
   But dimly imagined of man.

There once the opulent East,
   With sumptuous caravan
And blithe bazar and feast,
   Rejoiced in the gifts of life;
And love allured, and strife
   Was wine to the conquering strong.
There women with ardent eyes
   Drew souls to sacrifice,
And the day of work seemed long
   Till it brought the night of rest,
When the instruments of the dance
   Made the hours a happy trance;
And jewels were thrown to the best
   In wit or story or song.

The silver of temple bells
   Clove through the sunset gold,
Or else, in these cities old,
   Called the early to prayer,

Cities of Eld

When the swart, unhurrying throng
   Paced to their altars there;
The splendid pillars upsoared
   Circled with painted scenes
From the midst of the forest greens;
   And marbled fountains plashed
And swords processional flashed,
   When the gaping crowds stood fast,
Beholding some mighty lord
   Go by, with his pomp of state.

Alas, for the fall of fate!
   Look! there is nothing there;
Listen! no sound is heard,
   Save haply a vagrant bird
Or a wind-wail, or the blare
   Of thunder; — there is no worth
Of merchandise, no mirth,
   No lyric word of love;
Great, savage seams of earth
   Cover the marks thereof.
'Tis only but now and then
   That venturesome modern men
Set forth on a hard-won quest
   From the fresher world of the West,
To stand in that silent Vast
   And remember them of the Past.
'Tis scarcely more than a dream,
   This olden worship and lust,
This fragrance smothered in rust,
   This beauty of transient gleam;

Cities of Eld

    A symphony sunk to a moan,
       A famine after a feast ;
   The most are like to the least ;
       The towers are razed, are prone,
   Yea, all of the folk are dust
       And even their gods unknown.

A CHOPIN PRELUDE

A CERTAIN Chopin prelude once I heard.
Strive as I may to tell, no mortal word
Can all-express that music.   Like a bird
My soul went up the blue — the sweetest pain,
The deepest passion, love without a stain,
A high and holy yearning that had lain
Buried, did come in a white company,
In tremulous procession, unto me.
For an immortal moment I was free
O' the flesh, and leaped in spirit and was
    strong
With beauty, shaken by magic of that song.

THE WAYS RETURN

MANY the ways that man must fare,
    The roads run up and down ;
Some thrid the country hillsides fair,
    Some slink within the town.

Some tortuous are and hard to keep,
    But others slip along
Where gardens grow and fountains leap
    And speech is sweet, and song.

Some stretch away 'midst alien sights,
    'Midst strange, far-lying things ;
Others be near the native lights,
    Nor reck of journeyings.

And oh, the lingering, long quest,
    The stumblings, triumphs, pain,
The while man fares it east and west
    Ere he return again.

But one boon, one, is sure to be,
    How far soe'er he roam :
At last the wandering ways agree,
    At last they lead him home.

THE ELEMENTAL JOYS

THE elemental joys ! How far away
    And dim they seem, amidst the modern fret ;
The tumultuous probings, and the eyes tear-wet ;
The dark forever treading on the day !
        The elemental joys ! And yet,

Behold them close at hand ! The open sky,
    And all her sweep and thrill ; the open fire,
    Sleeking the body to its heart's desire ;
The white hands of the chosen home-mate —why,
        They all are goodly-nigh,

Nor is death any greedier than of old:
So, comrades, let us foot it free and bold,
    Win song and love and solace like a boy's —
        The elemental joys !

THE NORTH LIGHT
THE ARTIST SPEAKS

GIVE me the room with a clear north light
To paint my pictures in ;
For how may the artist paint aright,
   And meed eternal win,

Unless the sun come temperately
   Through the roof there, overhead ?
Yea, the clear north light is the light for me,
   As the dark is for the dead !

If I let the fervid south fierce shine
   On the creatures of my brush,
They are passion-warped, for the heat, like wine,
   Will set my blood a-rush ;

Whereas, the artist, like God on high,
   Must work in no hot whim ;
Aroused, yet calm, with a steady eye,
   While the centuries gaze at him.

There is love that lasts and a patience long
   In his forms and colors sure ;
And the light he needs, that he go not wrong,
   Is a high light, sane and pure.

When the great Thought comes and the gleam of
     Power,
   There is warmth divine in his soul;
But the labor drugs him hour by hour
   And far away is the goal ;

The North Light

So, for mastery, and the deed well done,
    He must cleanse his sight of all
The quick distempers bred in the sun
    That take weak men in thrall.

Must nurse the spark and the vision swift
    In the chastened light of the sky ;
That the work, though slow, have a heavenward lift,
    That the Beauty may not die.

In the place where the pictures have their birth
    Give me a north light clear,
With more of God and less of earth
    In the quiet atmosphere.

LIGHT AND SHADE

THIS one knows joy, and says: "Ah,
    Life is sweet!"
And sorrow this one: "Nay, 'tis drowned in
    tears."
Meanwhile, the picture is made all complete
    By God, great Chiaroscurist of the years,
Who uses light and shade, and in whose thought
The whole is clearly limned and calmly sought.

CHILD-PLAY

AS children play with toys,
   So men with hopes and fancies :
The little ones with romp and noise
   Build card-frail, gold romances ;
Their elders through the perilous years
Build dreams — and wake to toil and tears.

But, old or young the same,
   The glittering baubles please them ;
And be it fame or game,
   These make-believes release them
From iron circumstance, from drear
Realities that choke them here.

LIFE

FRIENDLY it stands, yon Inn upon the plain,
   And keen the lamps burn through the cryptic
     night.
  How jocund sound the voices, and how bright
The cheer ! how warm the housing from the rain !

The traveller, once arrived, forgets the long,
   Blank journey leading thither ; all the dim,
   Mysterious days are nothing now to him,
Seated amidst the food and wine and song.

But when, the reckoning paid, his comrades fled,
   He steps upon the road and moves away,
   His soul is puzzled sore — he cannot say
What Inn it was, or by whom tenanted.

THE ETERNAL FEMININE

FOREVER shall she beckon. Men may prate
Of custom, fashion, change, — still doth she
 call
To high endeavor ; dreams begotten thence
Turn with the day to deeds chivalric ; vows
Are pledged eternally before this shrine
Whose taper-lights are stars, whose choristers
Are souls bowed down with Beauty. Years on
 years
But dim the garments of the worshippers,
The light, the lure, are constant. All too brief
Is Time wherein to follow from afar
The Way of Wonder leading down to Love.
Look, at the alley-end she sways and smiles,
Fresh as a morn-birth, fair as paradise,—
Yet ancient as the moaning of the sea !

A WESTERN SCENE

THE land puts on a haggard look;
    For branchless boles of trees uprise
  In straggling groups, in tragic wise,
Black, weather-beaten, God-forsook.

Upon the plain, in high relief
    Against wide heaven, you may see
    Them flaunt spectacular misery,
Stamping a summer scene with grief.

Yet somewhile in the long ago
Blossomed and bloomed an Eden-show
Of beauty here — where now is this
Bleak picture of a wilderness?

THE MODERN SAINT

NO monkish garb he wears, no beads he tells,
    Nor is immured in walls remote from strife.
But from his heart deep mercy ever wells ;
    He looks humanely forth on human life.

In place of missals or of altar dreams,
    He cons the passioned book of deeds and days ;
Striving to cast the comforting sweet beams
    Of charity on dark and noisome ways.

Not hedged about by sacerdotal rule,
    He walks a fellow of the scarred and weak.
Liberal and wise his gifts ; he goes to school
    To Justice ; and he turns the other cheek.

He looks not holy ; simple is his belief ;
    His creed for mystic visions do not scan ;
His face shows lines cut there by others' grief,
    And in his eyes is love of brother-man.

Not self nor self-salvation is his care ;
    He yearns to make the world a sunnier clime
To live in ; and his mission everywhere
    Is strangely like to Christ's in olden time.

No mediæval mystery, no crowned,
    Dim figure, halo-ringed, uncanny bright.
A modern saint : a man who treads earth's ground,
    And ministers to men with all his might.

SEALED ORDERS

WE bear sealed orders o'er Life's weltered sea,
    Our haven dim and far ;
We can but man the helm right cheerily,
    Steer by the brightest star,

And hope that when at last the Great Command
    Is read, we then may hear
Our anchor song, and see the longed-for land
    Lie, known and very near.

BLACK OAKS

THE leaves of the black oak linger the winter through
In the woods of the wide Northwest; leech-like they cling
To the branch, and they nowise yield to blight and snow,
Presences dun and mystic; oft is the view
Framed in their subtle richness; oft they ring
Horizons else remote as the Long Ago.
The leaves of the black oak bide, and for me their grace
Has a conjuring touch of home, of a dear lost place;
I forget the plains, I behold New England's face.

HAYING-TIME

IN the meadows the men are haying:
   I can hear the creak of the cart,
I can see the play of the muscles,
   And the honest sweat outstart.

But the blue sky, calm and ample,
   With tranquil speech doth say:
" Why sweat, O ye tiny toilers,
   When your work is for a day?"

CHANGELESS

LOVE hath full many semblances : Now this
Fair face doth lure, now yonder smile re-
makes
A sorry world ; now at a mad-cap kiss
We build unstable dreams : the vision takes
A myriad forms, and hath the charm thereof. —
But ever, in the background, soareth Love,
One deathless creature poised beyond, above !

" IN SPEAKING OF THE LITTLE ONES WE LOVE "

IN speaking of the little ones we love
Our souls grow warm and tender : Young-of-
Years
So helpless seems, yet valiant, trusting all
It sees, and putting faith in the Unseen ;
Deeming the whole cold-hearted outer world
A mother-embrace, a bosom for its sleep.

We men are little ones before high God :
In pain, in sickness, and in moods that yearn
For consolation, or when we intrust
Our pigmy bodies to their night-still beds,
The spirit feels its youth and feebleness
And turns like any weak, perplexèd child
Toward home, toward father, mother, and the
things
Indwelling, known of old, and longed for still,
'Midst infinite barrenness and all unrest.

We men are little ones before high God :
The boasts of brain, the passions of the mind
Are nothing, set beside the one brief hour
Of faith re-born, calm dreams, and utter love.

GOSPELS

TWO Gospels there are of the years
   That haunt men, and follow them after :
And one is the Gospel of tears,
   The other the Gospel of laughter.

The Gospel of laughter is good,
   For it sweetens the gall of our sorrow ;
Therethrough is slow anguish withstood
   And the spirit trussed up for the morrow.

The Gospel of tears is divine,
   For it makes us draw closer together,
And shows us the beacon and sign
   Of souls, in Life's stormiest weather.

Two Gospels there are of the years,
   Rich-crowning our grief and our pleasure :
The Gospel of laughter, of tears,
   With meanings that man may not measure.

TRAVEL

I SIT in mine house at ease,
   Moving nor foot nor hand ;
Yet sail through unchartered seas
   And wander from land to land.

And though I may travel far,
   It is always well with me ;
I can come from an outmost star
   At a touch, at a call from thee.

THE QUEST OF SUMMER

I

I HAD been waiting long
  For its coming,
For the time of bird-song
  And the humming
Of the bees and the smell of May grass,
Till it seemed that the winter sleep never would pass
  To the buoyant bright waking of summer,
    Sweet comer,
With the mood of a love-plighted lass.

  But it came,
  In a garment of sensitive flame
In the west, and a royal blue sky overhead,
With exuberant breath and the bloom of all things
  Having wonders and wings,
  Being risen elate from the dead.
  Yea, it came with a flush
  Of pied flowers, and a turbulent rush
  Of spring-loosened waters, and an odorous hush
  At nightfall, — and then I was glad
With the gladness of one who for militant months
    has been sad.

  Then for days,
  In the warm noon haze,
In the freshness of morning or spirit-still mood of
    the night,
    My delight
Was wordless and deep, was a benison straight
    from my God ;

The Quest of Summer

    For the sky and the sod
Were marvels, and living a joy, and dun winter a myth;
    But therewith
Crept a change, — no swift spasm of nature, no death
Of brightness and beauty, but soberer drawing of breath
    That follows on rapture; no pall
Of sorrow, but splendid and bounteous Fall,
Whose veil is soft silver, who heralds a festival
    Of harvests and hopes and desires,
      Around whose fires
Dance satyrs and nymphs and young Bacchus the jocund, whose shapes
Are purply with time-mists and grapes.

    Then I knew
  How September's most opulent blue
  Must merge in October's calm gold,
    As ever of old;
A month thorough-thrilled with the prescience of ultimate pain;
    That again
Would follow November wind-writhen and sere,
  Then winter, a wild-mannered fere.
    So I said: "I will hasten from here,
I will win to what climes are more winsome and warm,
Where skyey beatitudes are, and no storm
May startle them out of their passionless norm
    Of peace;

The Quest of Summer

<blockquote>
Where release
From weathers shall last through each day of the seven,
So long as below is the earth and above is the heaven."
</blockquote>

So when the season came of hooded skies,
   Of wailing voices and of cheerless ways,
I ventured forth upon this sole emprise,
   Nor saw my mother-land for many days.

II

Soft slumbrous breathings of the enchanted noon
That drift and sift across the lapsed lagoon ;
The hush of heat, and for a constant tune
The languid silver swash of Southern seas.

The cocoa palms seem tranced upon the air
With cassia odorous ; all bright and bare
Of sails the sea ; the coral reefs gleam fair
Along the beach, and boom the big swart bees.

Here in this island-haunt a soul may rest
Like to a child upon the mother-breast,
Dreaming no dream that is not smooth and blest,
Nor waking save to solaces as dear.

Night follows noon, and then each star above
Looms like a moon and pulses life and love ;
The waters moan as moans a rapt white dove,
And whilom water-fowls make clamor clear.

The Quest of Summer

How long have I been here ? Ah, who can tell ?
The hours are but estrays of Time — no bell
Tinkles to warn the islanders ; but well
They know the day-dawn : It was yesteryear,

Perchance, or yesterday ; it matters not,
There are no hounding cares to make a blot
Upon Life's face, to rouse the trancèd spot
Into unease and bodings fraught with fear.

How can I e'er be sad, so bathed in bliss ?
Here is unceasing summer ; here, I wis,
One need but lie and watch the sky-line kiss
The waves, and pluck the poppy in the sand.

Unceasing summer, aye ; . . and far from home !
How many countless leagues across the foam
The sail-sick mariner must rock and roam
Before he sight the long-witholden land !

And there are icy wind and barren snow,
And here all tropic splendors bloom and blow ;
Then who would leave it, nor be loth to go
From pleasance such to breast a wintry clime ?

Lo, for the asking, lemons, mangoes, milk,
And berries, shedding fragrance ; soft as silk
The bed whereon I lie, the breezes ilk
That fan my face, the bath at morning-time.

The Quest of Summer

Below, a myriad colors on the earth,
Around, a shifting miracle, a birth
Of beauty new, and ever wonder-worth ;
Above, the great deep sapphire of the sky.

It were a marvel did a man regret
Within this June eternal : ah, but yet
I feel mine eyes north-gazing, sometimes wet.
Mayhap it is mere surfeit of delight,

Or is it love and longing for the lost
Keen raptures of a country tempest-tossed,
By all the savageries of nature crossed
And crowned with cold, as kings with circlets bright ?

Nay, ask me not ; but I must now away,
Seeking my native land, as wanderers may,
Homesick, and taught by every flawless day
How better than all else the old-time things.

I must away — so fetch my lithe canoe
To dare the foam and tread the sea-halls blue.
A swift farewell, O Isle of Dreams, to you,
O Southern Cross, see where in heaven it swings.

III

I came with the winds and the weather
    To the well-belovèd place,
And I recked not a rose-worth whether
    Sere winter had showed his face

The Quest of Summer

On the sea and the land,
    In the icy air,
Or whether the year was bland and fair:
All weather was seemly weather,
    Because it was homelike there.
In those sunshine isles of the Southern sea
The old keen joyance had slipt from me,
    I sated soon of the ceaseless boon
    Of drowsy days by the still lagoon.

But now my thoughts were interblent with birds
    And blandishments of morning; all the land
Was lovely past the putting it in words,
    Yet changeful as a maid who gives her hand,
But will not do it wantonly, for fear
It make her seem less dear.

So the secret was won forever,
    And I hugged it tight to my breast:
How the life all-summered, never
    Knows passion nor joy's behest.

How the spring change wakes to rapture
    The spirit so long asleep,
And the May month seems to capture
    A bliss that is twofold deep

When it follows hard on a sullen time
Of cheerless fields and of limping rhyme,
With a lyric thrill and a burst sublime.

The Quest of Summer

So my quest of summer was over ;
The time of corn and of clover,
  Of robin and rose and radiant hours,
Came to my door as a welcome guest,
  Welcome with birds and flowers,
And I feasted fine in the warmth and scent ;
But when 'twas o'er I was well content,
  Facing the sober fall with zest ;
    Nor winter frore
    Could evermore
Be aught but a rough-wayed friend to me, —
A friend who had preached high-heartedly
Courage, faith in the good-to-be.

    For the sweetest of all seasons
    Is that which follows pain,
    And the best of winter's reasons
    Is the summer here again.

ON THE LINE

A LITTLE picture hung — its peaceful stretch
Of sunny field; its glimpse of shady lane
Wherein the cattle, stragglers ponderous,
Made leisurely advance; its distant hills
That left the background dreamy, and above,
Beyond, the summer sky white-flecked with cloud, —
Dulled down and killed because on either side
Were canvases of other themes and tones.
The eye, confused by these so variant thoughts,
Must wander helplessly, nor stay to judge
The patient artist's meaning; so the small
And modest picture missed its due effect.

'Twas bought by one who had the seeing soul.
One day he showed it me within a room
Where all was harmonized to suit its mood.
I found it hard to think my memory
Had played me false, so foully disesteemed
The treasure that mine eyes must now behold:
The wealth of coloring, the breadth and range,
The worship breathing through and under all.

'Tis thus with men. Alive, they jostle past,
Shoulder to shoulder with some fellow-man
Who draws our gaze away. We hardly know
If they be gods or ghosts, so carelessly
We sense their presence. Death lifts up his hand
And beckons once; they follow, leave the crowd.

On the Line

We straight collect their words and scattered
   deeds,
Abstract our thoughts from off the busy world,
And study all that went to make them rare,
Until they stand disburdened and declared.
Then, next, we garnish up a pedestal,
Unused before, and lift their image high
For wise posterity in after-time
To humbly pause and view them, stern in stone.

CLEAR HEAVENS

THE sky is wind-swept, and the golden air,
 Rain-washed, is crystal-clear and keen to
 breathe.
The hills since yesterday have shaken off
Their dim aloofness, and uprise so near,
Clean cut and purple 'gainst the brow of morn,
They startle you. There is a brilliancy
Set like a seal on earth and heaven; it seems
As if all Nature made her ready for
Some festival, some august guest to come
And tarry for a day. Some joy-to-be
Haunts in the field, inhabits all the woods,
And thrids the blue; nor e'en night's darker
 mood
Dispels the strong illusion: since the stars
Shine brighter than their wont, and breezes blow
The message, "Patience; it will all come true."

TWO BARDS

A BARD who wrote in staves
    Once made a heathen hymn.
It had this stern refrain,
    That moved as though in pain:
"The under-glimpse of graves
    Makes the sea grim."

A south-land singer sung
    With happy heart and free.
    The living, not the dead,
    He dealt with, and he said:
"The world is glad and young,
    And good to me."

And ever since, mankind
    Is shuttled back and forth
    Between these singers twain
    Of glad and sad refrain:—
The southland warm and kind,
    The bitter north.

PLAINT OF THE PINE

I FOUND a pine that shot its solemn bole
   Twice fifty feet against the summer sky
From out a sunless gorge ; and sad of soul
   It seemed, until I sought to question why ;
   Whereat the tree moaned darkly — made this
     strange reply :

"I am troubled betimes, I am sad in my sleep,
Foreboding the day I shall stagger and leap
And tremble through tempests o'er seas that are
   deep.

"They will fashion me forth for a ship ; they will
   make
My stature and girth but a mock ; they will break
My branches and rend me for merchanting's
   sake.

"Eternal unease shall be portioned to me,
A creature firm rooted and fain so to be, —
Eternal unease on the shifting, loud sea.

"For each to his nature ; and mine is to grow
Tall, sombre, and steadfast, and gravely a-row
With brothers as grave, while the centuries go.

"I am troubled betimes, I am sorely oppressed,
As I ponder and dream on my mother-earth's
   breast,
With a fear of the ocean, that knoweth not rest."

TRAGEDIES

TWO kinds there are : the one theatric, bold,
    A murder, maybe, horrible to see,
Lives lost by fire or flood, and bodies cold
    That speak some tale of awful agony ;

The other, mumming 'neath a milder name :
    A human soul that as the days go by
Sinks deeper down into some pit of shame,
    Yet knows the stars shine silvery and high.

FLASHES

A FLASH of the lightning keen!
And lo! we know that, miles on miles,
The dim, lost land is lying green.
It brims our heart with joy, the whiles,
To see that through the thick night-screen
Full many a meadow smiles and smiles.

A flash from the poet's brain!
The meaning of the many years,
That mazeful seemed, grows very plain;
The level lands of gloom and tears
Hint holy heights, turn bright again;
The night a transient thing appears.

LAUREL

ALONG the road in the month of June,
   With all the roses in their prime,
The laurel blooms and hears the tune
   Of all the birds, for 'tis their time
     Of fullest, fairest singing.

And no man meets awake, a-dream,
   A daintier pink on lady-cheek
Than paints those clustered cups that seem
   Like nuns demure and over-meek,
     So close together clinging.

Some flowers are for city walks,
   And some o'er love's light lattice climb;
And some are noisome on their stalks,
   While others scent the summer time
     In quiet garden closes.

But most of all, methinks, I love
   Along some road of solitude
To see the laurel, flower of
   A simpler yet a sweeter mood
     Than any mood of roses!

MARY MAGDALEN

AT dawn she sought the Saviour slain,
To kiss the spot where he had lain
And weep warm tears, like Spring-time rain ;

When lo! there stood, unstained of death,
A man that spake with slow, sweet breath ;
And " Master ! " Mary answereth.

From out the far and fragrant years,
How sweeter than the songs of seers
That tender offering of tears !

PICTURES

I

A PALLID nun, by serge made doubly pale,
   Stoops to the pavement for a red, ripe leaf
Dropt from a tree, and smiles beneath her veil
   In thinking this may soothe a sick child's grief.

II

A cool contralto voice that calms the soul,
   As night-wind calms the pulses hot with pain;
And, crouching in a seat, the grave her goal,
   A wanton grown a simple girl again.

III

A street musician singing of the sea
   Amidst the shipping of a smoke-wrapt town ;
Until a soft south breeze from Italy
   Touches the cheek, and fairer skies float down.

THE DREAM AND THE WAKING

A DREAM slipped out of a wood :
  Ah, foolish dream !
You found no other good
  By stile, by stream
  (So would it surely seem),
Like to the cool sweet wood
  With odors all ateem.

But stay ! A slight girl stood,
  White browed, with claspèd hands,
  Down in the meadow lands,
    Down in the meadow there,
    And fair, ah fair !
  The dream, the wood forsaking,
    Wise in his way, full wise,
    Stopped because of her eyes,
  Stopped and found fair waking, —
The dream slipped out of the wood
And found a better good :
  The sweet pine haunts forsaking,
  He passed to a happy waking,
    To life in a maiden's eyes.
    Ah, he was wise !

LIFE AND SONG

LIFE is the seed one soweth,
　　Song is the springing flower;
Life is the tear that floweth,
　　Song is the happy hour.

For as the seed must tarry
　　Under the chilly mould,
Only to swell and carry
　　Savor in every fold;

And as the tear prepareth
　　Hearts for the coming bliss,
And by the pain it beareth
　　Widens the soul for this;

So will a seed of sorrow
　　Blossom my life along;
So will a tearful morrow
　　Write me a deeper song.

INTERPRETATION

A SORROWER went his way along,
   And I heard him sing and say :
"The noon is bright, but soon the night
   Will come, the grave of the day."

Then I smiled to hear his woful song
   And sent this word for nay :
"The noon is bright, but the blackest night
   Cradles another day."

THE NATIONAL AIR

I SAT at home and heard an air
  Played slow and solemnly;
But slow or swift, I did not care,
   It nothing spake to me.

'Twas hackneyed, stale, I could but smile
   To think how some will cheer,
Yea, dauntless tramp through death's defile,
   If but that song be near.

In after days I heard again
   This anthem rolling grand;
But now I sat 'midst foreign men
   Within a foreign land.

And in a trice my soul took flame,
   My blood was fire in me;
I trembled at my country's name
   With love and fealty!

A PRELUDE

LITTLE conjurer of keys,
You shall play me, and you please,
From the masters, music-blessed,
Playing what I love the best:

Something sweet of Schumann's make,
Something sad for Chopin's sake;
Then a waltz with gayer graces
Born of Liszt and pleasant places.

Next, to sway my dreaming soul,
Play a Schubert barcarole;
And, to wake me from the trance,
Just a tricksy Spanish dance.

Now a fugue of Bach's, a song
Weaving thoughts of right and wrong;
And a thing of airy tone
That belongs to Mendelssohn.

A sonata-strain whose grief
Gave Beethoven's heart relief;
Last a melody divine
From the soul of Rubinstein.

Playing thus, the warp of life,
Dark of hue and sorrow-rife,
Shall be gladdened fold on fold
With a woof of sunny gold,
Woven from your melodies,
Little conjurer of keys.

IN THE GRASS

I AM one with waving things,
   Lying in the grass to-day;
Harkening to the song that rings
   When the robin has his say.
   Cares and crosses fall away,
As the raindrops from the wings
   Of a bird. Amidst the hay
I am one with waving things.

I am one with waving things,
   For I do not speak aloud.
Nay, the peace that silence brings
   Keeps me like a windless cloud,
   Till I clean forget the crowd
Cityward, whose happenings
   Oft and o'er my soul have cowed,
Dull and dead to waving things.

I am one with waving things,
   For I lie and brood and grow
Very full of bygone springs,
   Very full of dreams that flow
   Saplike after winter snow;
Brother to the bird that sings
   For a cause he may not know
I am one with waving things.

THE POET TO THE CLOUD

    SOFT white cloud in the sky,
       Wise are you in your day :
One side turned toward God on high,
   One toward the world alway.
Soft white cloud, I too
Would bear me like to you.

So might I secrets learn
   From heaven, and tell to men ;
And so might their spirits beat and burn
   To make it their country then.
Soft white cloud, make mine
Such manner of life as thine.

A STORM

KEEN fiery furrows in the skyward field :
The thunder's big black voice sounds loud and long,
The wind, wild witch, has fitful shrieked and reeled
From east to west, as stung by sense of wrong ;
While from a tree, 'midst goodly green concealed,
A fearless bird carols a careless song.

THE LILY

THY loveliness is meek and free
   From arrogance, and yet I find
A certain stately pride in thee
   That wakens revery in my mind.

And well I ween why it is so! —
   A lily once the Master took
His lesson from, then let it go,
   But first he blessed it with a look.

Ah! who can doubt the flower was thrilled
   With tremblings strange, and raised its head
With joy, its lovesome body filled
   With sense of what the Master said?

And lilies since, forevermore,
   Do hold them high, do bear them well,
Do raise their cups more proudly, for
   The lily of the parable.

THE MUSIC STRAIN

"MUSIC strain, where do you go,
When you hush and vanish so?"

"Sure, I only take my rest
In a spot that's beauty-blest."

"Music strain, may mortals too
Gird them up and go with you?"

"Nay, for I am all divine,
And my country is not thine."

"Music strain, will death reveal
All the bliss you make us feel?"

"Mortal, listen, love me well,
And together we may dwell."

"Yes, but when, O subtle song!
For the waiting seems so long?"

"I will house thee safe and sure,
When thy love is perfect-pure."

"Ah, it seems I cannot stay
For the break of such a day!"

"Mortal, it is wondrous near;
Hope and hark, and have no fear."

A MADRIGAL

APRIL eyes, April eyes,
   Alight with laughter,
Where is the lucky swain
Who in those blue orbs twain
May read the answer plain
   He would be after?

April eyes, April eyes,
   Fast brimming over,
Will he not come again?
Ah, after blue skies rain,
After brief pleasure pain;
   Love is a rover.

GYPSIES

CHILDREN of the lost tribe, home-banished ones,
Aliens and outcasts, — but rich dowered in
The sun and shade and all the leagues of air,
Ye are a sign and symbol of the race —
The restless, unappeasèd race of man —
Whose roots, mayhap, strike deep in some dear soil
Long lost, but whose unsure and questing feet
Wander, the while his eye that scans the blue
Welcomes new vistas, and his seeking soul
Camps for a night, — but with the morn's first sounds
Girds up, to take the old eternal trail
Godward, to find the Tent of Peace, wherein
All nomads relish the home-keeping ways, —
Clan of the wander-weary, tamed at last.

A LEGEND OF THE MOON

NIGHTLONG I yearned so madly toward the moon,
Meseemed she whispered low the ancient rune
Of her past history — as strange a word
On life and death and doom as e'er I heard:
So wondrous strange it did my soul constrain
      To tell the tale again.

A legend this of eld and other spheres:
In times before the dawn of human deeds
On earth, life swarmed upon the mystic moon,
Where now is stony silence, — ages ere
Chaldæans probed the riddles of the sky,
Or swart Egyptians slumbered in their tombs.
The air was sweet for breathing; all the ways
Trembled with speech of folk or song of birds
Blithe-mooded — cities clung along the slopes
Or darkened on the plains, the land teemed tilth;
Wide-yawing ships swept over seas whose names
Are immemorial; wars raged red, and Art
Thrust temples white where once the wild beast prowled,
And in her limbec poured men's grosser thoughts
Distilling dreams and subtle dews divine.

The moon-man is the sole possessor now
In those vast regions. He is known of all
The children from their birth-while: him you see
On cloud-clear nights (if you will patient peer)
Sitting upon a round of massy stone
Within a great grey desert where the light

Is ghostly wan.   Upon his face is writ   *A Legend of*
Unuttered agonies of things long lost   *the Moon*
Yet keen remembered : rugged is his brow,
And in his eyes a Horror blackly broods.
But how he came, and why he sits alone,
Behooves the telling — list, it happened thus :

Æons ago the gods had mind to make
(For pleasure of their august realms) a world
Of beings fleshed in bodies, but with souls
Whose spark was like their own.   Whereon they
   glanced
About those primal heavens, and saw afar
A little globe that wheeled a constant course
Through space.   And since it looked a seemly
   spot
To nourish life, they spoke the fiat — then
A cry of young humanity was heard
Upon the moon.   But ere the word was said
That gave this dubious gift of living, lo!
The gods did set a bound to lunar years,
To lives that dwell thereon : So long a time
(They swore) as human face should look on face
With faith and kindliness, might breath be drawn,
And no whit after, — changeless the decree.
Herein was shown most meet desire that love
Be Lord of Life, that neither loveless crime
Nor lust should harden hearts until that men,
Wrapt up in self-hood, let their brothers go
To bliss or bane unnoted : hence the law.

A Legend of the Moon Then ages fled and kingdoms waxed and waned
In that moon-country with the march of time.
But life, that first bloomed freshly, like a flower
Sweet-natured with the air and rain and sun,
Grew weed-like, noisome, foul. Thereon the gods
Sent plagues to scourge : — the moon-folk heeded not.
Then certain of the cities most engorged
In fleshly ways, were smote ; as afterwhile
The earth saw cities stricken in their pride :
Sodom, Gomorrah, wide-walled Babylon,
Whose monarch was anhungered with the kine.
The people paused, but soon, emboldened, turned
Unto their idol of the cloven hoof ;
And over all the land men's eyes were glazed
Toward Love, and greedy but for sordid gain.
Now came the gods to council, and the law,
The ancient screed wherein was set the terms
Of habitation on the doomèd orb,
Was gravely conned : and it was plain to see
That total, fell destruction must ensue,
If they would keep their word inviolate.
And so with ponderous, grim debate they chose
To send a rain of fire from heaven to scorch
The world of men and women on the moon :
Save only one, a hermit hoary, who
Had all his days lived wisely, sought the light
And loved his fellows. *Leave him to his prayer,
And suffer him to make a gentler end
Whenso he wills,* the mighty mandate read.

So was it done : one awful day and night   *A Legend of*
(Uncalendared within that dateless land)   *the Moon*
The liquid flame licked down, and ceasing, left
Ashes and bones and formless waste, wherefrom
The some-time splendor of a world had been.
And he, the moon-man, whom the children know,
The childlike hermit of this elder race,
Was left alone.
         And now a bleak despair
And sorrow nipped his blood, and he was fain
To perish by his cave. But erst at eve
He stood within a strange and windless plain
And with lack-lustre gaze beheld where shone
Through trackless leagues of space the clustered
   lights
Of constellations, idly looked upon
Fixed stars of vibrant flickerings, did mark
The changeless glow of planets in their path,
Argent or gold or ruddy-faced like Mars :
And saw, or deemed he saw, or dreamed he saw,
A shape, that moved upon one orb, the earth,
A silver cirque that lit the nether sky.
Whereat a tremor shook his spirit lax,
And it grew tense : his soul was hung upon
That shifting thing, that blot against a star,
Until he knew it for a mortal man
And wept, and cried aloud, to think that he
Was less companionless.
             Thereafter, though
His lot was gruesome and his sorrows lead
Against his heart, a kind of pensive calm

A Legend of the Moon

Settled within him as he watched our orb
Thro' years and sweeping cycles, e'en to Now.
Nor had he will to die, because of this
Weird watch and ward, this brooding over us.
Nay, once he even smiled a moment's space,
Beholding how a deed of charity
Was done a lonesome soul : and once his eyes
Looked dreamy in their sockets gaunt, because
An earth-poet's fancy dubbed yon yellow ball
*An octoroon beside those slim white girls,
The stars.* But most his mood set sorrowward,
And most his sighs were like the homeless wind
That moans about the gables in the night.
Sleep does not visit him from month to month :
Mandrake nor poppy may not lure his eyes
From earthward quest ; awake and sad, he seems
To yearn within his poised and dizzy haunt
For easement of the warning in his mind
To us of earth, lest we let Love be lost
— That crystal candle 'midst the bogs of hate
And guile and lack-of-Love and lusts untamed —
As did his kindred, so their sorry case
Be ours : remembering that the self-same gods
Shaped him and us and all.
                          Be such his thoughts
Or no, he keeps his vigil, and his front
Looks dumbly down, — while I upgaze at him
And wonder if his brain be not distraint
With horrid weight of memory. Shall he find
A final solace for a fate forlorn,
And meet with us upon some higher sphere
To commerce once again with human kind

By touch of hand and mouth and interchange *A Legend of*
Of words, a long withholden boon to him? *the Moon*
So far the moon has whispered : here she stays
Her silver secrets, leaves me unappeased.

Along came Science in a surly mood
Of introspection, harked awhile, nor spake,
Frowned ominously, and then at length found
   speech,
That made but tatters of my peopled moon,
The mid-air ship that bore my single fleece
Of story. *'Tis a lie*, quoth he, *for ne'er*
Since chaos was there breath on yonder orb
Nor moving wight, nor sound of speech nor song
To make the mountains merry and the plains
Vital and thick with voices: None but babes
And sucklings can be fooled with such a myth.
Whereat mine answer : *Men are children still,*
And love their legends and their wonder-tales.
Moreover, came the record not from heaven,
From very heaven upon a cloudless night?
So, Science, leave me to my conjuring
Of moons and mortals and of olden days.

www.ingramcontent.com/pod-product-compliance
Lightning Source LLC
Chambersburg PA
CBHW020325090426
42735CB00009B/1411